INVENTORS

ALEXANDER GRAHAM BELL

PAUL JOSEPH
ABDO & Daughters

Published by Abdo & Daughters, 4940 Viking Drive, Suite 622, Edina, Minnesota 55435.

Printed in the United States.

Cover illustration and icon: Kristen Copham
Interior photos: Bettmann, pages 5, 23, 24, 26
                            Wide World Photos, pages 11, 20, 28
Photo colorization: Professional Litho

Edited by Julie Berg

Library of Congress Cataloging-in-Publication Data

Joseph, Paul, 1970-
Alexander Graham Bell / Paul Joseph.
    p.   cm. — (Inventors)
  Includes index.
  Summary: Sketches the life of the man who at the age of twenty-nine was responsible for the invention of the telephone.
  ISBN 1-56239-632-3
  1. Bell, Alexander Graham, 1847-1922. 2. Inventors--United States--Biography--Juvenile literature. [1. Bell, Alexander Graham, 1847-1922. 2. Inventors.] I. Title. II. Series: Inventors (Series)
TK6143.B4J67 1996
621.385'092—dc20
[B]   95-51272
                                                              CIP
                                                               AC

Contents

The Telephone

The ringing of the telephone is a very familiar sound. Today, many homes have two or three telephones.

The telephone is used for many different reasons: you can call a friend to come over and play, talk to a relative who lives far away, you can even use it to connect your computer to an online service. In emergencies, you can dial three numbers and reach the police or fire department in seconds. It is difficult to imagine life without the telephone.

Before the 20th century, people could not communicate with others in far-off places. This all changed because of Alexander Graham Bell. Thanks to him, it has become much easier to stay in touch with anyone in the world.

Opposite page:
Alexander Graham Bell.

The Early Years

Alexander Bell was born in Edinburgh, Scotland, on March 3, 1847. He was named after his grandfather, who shared the same birthday. Bell's father was also named Alexander. His middle name was Melville.

Young Alexander, who went by Aleck, was not given a middle name. So when he was 11 years old he decided to give himself one. After meeting a family friend from Cuba named Graham, Aleck decided that would be a perfect middle name. From then on he was known as Alexander Graham Bell.

As a young boy, Aleck was always **curious**, which sometimes got him into trouble. One of his earliest memories was of getting lost while on a family outing. Aleck wandered into a wheat field and put his ear to the ground. He wanted to know if wheat made a sound while it grew. He listened carefully but could not hear anything. He decided to return to his family, but got lost.

Then he heard his father cry out, "Aleck! Aleck!"

By listening to his father's booming voice, Aleck determined which direction to go. This made him more **curious** about sound.

Aleck had a remarkable gift for sounds and **tones**. His interest in sound was not surprising. Both his father and grandfather were speech teachers. They made the study of sound their life's work.

Aleck was also an excellent piano player. He could listen to a song once, then play it on the piano. His mother, Eliza, encouraged him to play. Though she was deaf, Eliza was a good pianist.

Aleck and his mother had a close relationship. While others spoke to her through a rubber ear tube, Aleck would not. He discovered that by speaking in low **tones** close to her forehead, she could understand what he was saying.

Aleck had two brothers, Melville, who was older, and Edward, who was younger. Eliza taught her three sons grammar, spelling, reading, and math at home.

A Talented Family

In the mid-1800s, people did not have television, computers, or radios. Families had to entertain themselves.

Everyone in the Bell family was talented. When they gathered in their house at night, the boys and their father would sing Scottish songs.

Because of her **deafness,** Eliza could not sing along. Instead, she would accompany her family on the piano. At times, Aleck would play a **duet** with his mother while his father played his flute.

Neighbors would come to the house to be entertained by the talented Bell family. When the singing and music ended, Melville would begin his magic show. The night would usually end with the three brothers doing **dramatic** readings of Shakespeare, Charles Dickens, and many other classic authors.

Aleck and His Animals

By the time he was ten, Aleck and his brothers were attending regular school. Aleck was not a good student, especially compared to his brothers. Aleck would rather practice music or sounds than study Latin and Greek. As for math, Aleck cared only for the **theory**. He made many mistakes when it came to the actual **arithmetic**.

In class, Aleck's mind wandered. It was hard for him to **concentrate**. He wanted to do so much more.

After school, Aleck enjoyed working on sounds and scientific matters. He would collect plants and dead animals, including mice, toads, rabbits, dogs, and cats, and **dissect** them.

Alexander Graham Bell experiments with his dog.

Aleck even **experimented** with his dog. By gently pressing on his dog's mouth and voice box, he could make noises that sounded like "How are you, Grandma?" Aleck's family could not believe how he did this.

Aleck Moves to London

Aleck finished high school when he was 15. Because his grades were so bad, Aleck would not join his brothers in college. His parents didn't know what to do with him.

Aleck's father wanted his son to do something important with his life. So he sent Aleck to live with Grandpa Bell in London, England. Aleck thought it couldn't possibly be any fun living in London, but he went anyway.

Aleck boarded the train. As it went south from Scotland through England to the city of London, Aleck thought about how he was going to miss his family, especially his mother. But Aleck knew deep down that the move to London would be good for him.

Aleck's grandfather was very smart and well-known throughout London for being an excellent speech teacher and author. He would help Aleck with his schooling. But Aleck was embarrassed because he didn't feel he was very smart. His grandfather changed all that by making school and learning a lot of fun. Aleck soon loved studying.

Aleck continued to play the piano. But his favorite hobby was reading and writing. He even wrote a play. His reading included **classics**, but many of his books were about speech and sound, written by his grandfather.

Aleck was grateful to his grandfather. Not only did he learn his lessons well, he learned about life. The one year in London with his grandfather changed Aleck from a boy to a man.

After a year in London, Aleck returned home. He was happy to see his family again. But something was missing. In London, he was treated like an adult. Now he was just another child in the house. He decided to get a job.

Aleck applied for a job teaching music and speech in town. Although only 16, he had enough music skills to teach anyone. And with his father and grandfather known throughout **Great Britain** as excellent speech teachers, he was easily hired.

Aleck loved teaching and was very good at it. The students respected him and liked his teaching style. The next year he was promoted to assistant master because of his fine work. In his spare time, he continued to read and do sound **research**. He was constantly thinking and remained **curious**.

Sad Days For the Bell Family

In 1865, Aleck's grandfather died. Aleck was very sad. He knew that without his grandfather's patience and love, he would never be teaching and doing the things he loved. Aleck never forgot what his grandfather had done for him.

The Bells decided to move to London. There, Aleck got a job teaching **deaf** children, something he truly loved. He taught visible speech, a way of communicating with the deaf. This method was invented by his father. It took over 15 years of **research** and study before it was complete. All three boys learned the technique and were teaching it. **Scientists** applauded the Bells' great work.

In 1867, another tragedy struck the Bell
household. Edward died of **tuberculosis**. This
disease killed many people during the 19th century.
Three years later, Melville died of the same disease.
The family was very sad. Aleck could not
understand why his brothers had to die.

Soon, Aleck began to get sick. Fearing the
worst, his parents took no chances. They decided
to move to North America where the climate was
healthier for Aleck.

The family settled on a farm in Brantford,
Ontario, Canada. Aleck began to get healthy. He
enjoyed farm work and the weather. But he wanted
to teach again and perform **experiments.** He also
wanted to invent a way in which sound could travel
through wires. This would help people
communicate.

Aleck Meets Watson

While Aleck's father was in Boston giving speeches, Sarah Fuller, who ran the public day school for **deaf** children, asked if he wanted to teach there. Aleck's father said he was too busy, but his son might be interested in the job. Aleck gladly accepted the offer.

Boston was great for Aleck. He loved the hectic city. There was so much to explore. When he wasn't teaching, he would visit libraries and attend lectures. Best of all, there were **scientists** and educators who worked in the area of sound. He could listen and learn from these very smart people. It was the perfect place for a person who wanted to be an inventor.

Alexander Graham Bell's

1847
Born March 3 in Edinburgh, Scotland.

1871
Moves to the U.S. to teach deaf students in Boston.

1872
Starts a school for the deaf in Boston.

1873
Begins teaching at Boston University.

1880
Helps start *Science* magazine.

1882
Becomes a U.S. citizen.

1886
Introduces the first cylinder which forms the basis of the modern phonograph.

Life & Invention Timeline

1876
Introduces the telephone to the world.

1877
Marries Mabel Hubbard.

1877
Organizes the Bell Telephone Company.

1898
Becomes president of the National Geographic Society.

1917
Develops the hydrodome—the fastest boat in the world.

1922
Dies August 2 in Baddeck, Nova Scotia, Canada.

Detail Area

MASSACHUSETTS • Boston

The Bell home in Brantford, Ontario.

As a teacher, Aleck excelled in every area. The following year, he started his own school. He had different ideas about teaching and wanted to use them. His plan was to train teachers of **deaf** students. At night, he continued his **experiments**, hoping to someday make a machine that **transmitted** sound.

In Boston, Aleck met his future assistant, Tom Watson. Watson worked in an electric shop with many different inventors and knew much about **electricity**. The two men hit it off right away.

Watson was impressed with the way Aleck could come up with ideas and never stopped thinking. Sometimes he would come to Watson's house in the middle of the night with ideas.

Aleck was equally impressed with Watson. Aleck wasn't good when it came to **mechanics**. He couldn't believe he could play a piano so well when he was "all thumbs." The two were about to make a great team.

The Telephone is Born

Aleck quit teaching and devoted all his time to inventing. Aleck and Watson worked day and night on their **experiments.** They still were trying to make a **telegraph**. They worked with tuning forks, wires, and batteries. Because Aleck had such a sharp and sensitive ear, he could easily adjust the tuning forks.

After much frustration, a breakthrough happened. When Watson tightened a screw too tight, Aleck heard a strange sound on his end of the telegraph. Aleck ran into Watson's room filled with excitement. Because of that strange sound, Aleck knew they could also send speech across the wire. The two inventors were elated. The invention of the telephone was now on its way.

Alexander Graham Bell's first telephone.

Aleck and Watson worked into the night. Aleck came up with a drawing for the "telephone," which comes from two Greek words: tele, meaning "far off" and phone, meaning "sound." Watson had the model made the next day.

The two inventors worked nonstop on the **telegraph** and telephone. They rented out a two-room apartment where they worked, ate, and slept. They rarely went outside or slept, preferring to work 20-hour days. They got the patent for the telegraph. But what they were really working on was the telephone.

"*Mr. Watson, come here, I want you!*" *were the first words spoken over a telephone. Mr. Watson rushed in shouting: "Mr. Bell, I heard every word!*"

After working a long time, it finally happened on March 10, 1876. Watson was in one room and Aleck in the other. Watson lifted the receiver to his ear and moments later heard the first telephone message in history.

Aleck's voice came over the wire loud and clear. "Mr. Watson, come here. I want you!" Watson ran into the room. The two inventors could not believe what had just happened. Twenty-nine-year-old Alexander Graham Bell had just come up with the invention that would change the world.

Alexander Graham Bell speaks into his new invention.

Aleck Changes the World

For the next few years, Aleck traveled the country demonstrating his telephone. People came from everywhere to see this remarkable invention. He even was invited to England where he showed it to the Queen. She was so impressed, she wanted to buy the two telephones that Aleck had brought along.

By 1915—nearly 40 years after the first phone call—many people had telephones. Lines crisscrossed the country side. But never had a coast-to-coast call been made. Aleck sat next to his phone in New York. Nearly 3,000 miles (4,800 km) away in California, Tom Watson sat next to his

phone. Would Aleck's voice carry that far? Again Watson heard the familiar words loud and clear: "Mr. Watson, come here. I want you!"

Throughout his life, Alexander Graham Bell continued to work on many inventions such as the photophone, which transmitted speech without wires. He invented a device that aided the lungs of **respiratory** patients called a vacuum jacket. He invented the metal detector and much more.

Although he made a huge difference in everyone's life with the invention of the telephone, he was most proud of his dedicated work with the **deaf** which he continued until his death on August 1, 1922.

Opposite page: Alexander Graham Bell makes the first New York-Chicago telephone call.

Glossary

arithmetic (uh-RITH-muh-tik) - The type of mathematics that deals with adding, subtracting, multiplying, and dividing numbers.

classic - A book that is written by an author of great excellence.

communication (kuh-mew-nih-KAY-shun) - To give or exchange information or news by speaking, writing, or using symbols.

concentrate (KAHN-sen-trait) - To pay close attention.

curious (CURE-ee-us) - Very eager to know and learn things.

deaf - Not able, or only partly able to hear.

dramatic - Very exciting; full of action or feeling.

electricity (ee-lek-TRIS-ih-tee) - A current or power.

experiment (ek-SPARE-uh-ment) - The process of testing in order to discover.

Great Britain - The countries of England, Scotland, and Wales; the largest island in Europe.

mechanics (muh-CAN-iks) - The process of building or repairing electrical machines.

receiver (ree-SEE-ver) - A part of the telephone held to the ear that receives sound.

research - A careful look for facts or truth; to investigate.

respiratory (RESS-pruh-tor-ee) - Having to do with breathing.

scientists (SIGH-en-tists) - A person who has expert knowledge of some branch of science.

telegraph (TELL-uh-graph) - A way of sending coded messages over wires by means of electricity.

theory (THEAR-ee)- An explanation based on observation.

tone - Any sound considered with reference to its quality, pitch, strength or source.

transmit - To pass along.

tuberculosis (too-bur-kew-LOW-sis) - A disease that destroys various tissues of the body, but most often the lungs.

Index